Christmas Duet Fun Book

O Come Little Children

Melody

O Come Little Children

Harmony

4 Bring a Torch, Jeanette, Isabella

Bring a Torch, Jeanette, Isabella

Jolly Old St. Nick

Melody

Jolly Old St. Nick

Harmony

8 O Come, O Come Emmanuel

O Come, O Come Emmanuel

Harmony

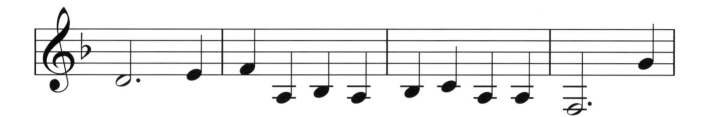

10 Ding Dong Merrily on High

Melody

Ding Dong Merrily on High

Harmony

silent Night

Melody

Silent Night

Harmony

Jingle Bells

Jingle Bells

Harmony

Fine

D.C. al Fine

O Come All Ye Faithful

Melody

O Come All Ye Faithful

Harmony

18 Angels We Have Heard on High

Melody

Angels We Have Heard on High

We Three Kings

Melody

We Three Kings

Harmony

Joy to the World

Joy to the World

24 Hark, the Herald Angels Sing

Hark, the Herald Angels sing

Harmony

Up on the Housetop

Up on the Housetop

Toyland

Melody

Toyland

O Holy Night (p. 1)

O Holy Night (p. 1)

O Holy Night (p. 2)

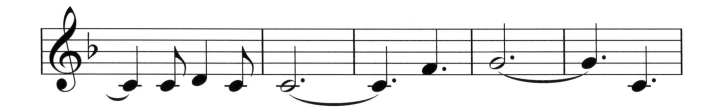

O Holy Night (p. 2)

Away in a Manger

Melody

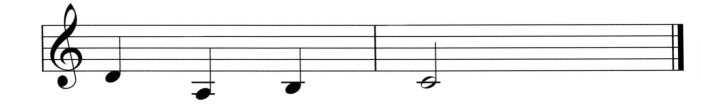

Away in a Manger

36 Go Tell It on the Mountain

Melody

Go Tell It on the Mountain

Harmony

The First Noel

Melody

The First Noel

Harmony

I Have a Little Dreidel

Melody

I Have a Little Dreidel

Harmony

Dreidel Turn

(S'vivon)

Melody

Dreidel Turn
(S'vivon)

Harmony

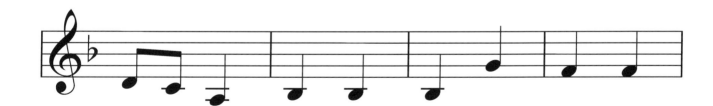

Hannukah Song

44

Melody

Hannukah song

Harmony

Made in United States
Troutdale, OR
12/08/2024

26095864R00027